The Civil Rights Movement

Researching American History

introduced and edited by
Pat Perrin

NAACP lawyers who won the Supreme Court on school desegregation included George E.C. Hayes, Thurgood Marshall, and James Nabrit. In 1967, Thurgood Marshall (center) became the first African American to serve on the Supreme Court.

Discovery Enterprises, Ltd.
Carlisle, Massachusetts

All rights reserved. No part of this book may be reproduced, stored in a retrieval system, or transmitted in any form or by any means, electronic, mechanical, photocopied, recorded, or otherwise, without prior written permission of the authors or publisher, except for brief quotes and illustrations used for review purposes.

First Edition © Discovery Enterprises, Ltd., Carlisle, MA 2003

ISBN: 1-57960-081-6

Library of Congress Catalog Card Number

10 9 8 7 6 5 4 3 2 1

Printed in the United States of America

Subject Reference Guide:

Title: *The Civil Rights Movement*
Series: *Researching American History*
introduced and edited by Pat Perrin

Credits:

Cover art: © Cartoon by Herblock, *Washington Post*, 1963.

Hate Crimes Today: An Age-old Foe in Modern Dress, pp. 51-56, used with permission of the American Psychological Association, Washington, D.C. 1998.

All other illustrations credited where they appear in the text.

Contents

About the Series 4
   Reading the Historical Documents 4
Introduction: Civil Rights 5
   Civil Rights Chronology 6
The Early 20th Century 8
   Lynching 8
   Mark Twain and Lyncherdom 8
   Two Philosophies and Two Approaches 10
   Booker T. Washington Protests 11
   The Original Protest Song 12
   Breaking Baseball's Color Barrier 13
   Integrating the Military 14
Ideas, Organizations, and People 15
   Nonviolence 15
   The NAACP 16
   SCLC 16
   COFO 17
   SNCC 17
   CORE 17
   Black Nationalism and Black Power 18
Desegregating Schools 19
   Brown v. Board of Education—1950–1954 19
   White Protest 21
   Integrating Central High 22
   A Central High Diary 23
   Central High School Newspaper 25
   James Meredith in Mississippi 26
Desegregating Transportation 27
   1956 Montgomery Bus Boycott 28
   Violence and Nonviolence in Montgomery 29
   Freedom Rides 30
   Mob Violence Unchecked 31
   Mobs in Montgomery 31
Desegregating Public Dining 32
   Diane Nash's Fear and Determination 36
Marching for Freedom 38
   Martin Luther King, Jr. on Why 39
   The March on Washington 41
   Marching for Voting Rights 42
   King Awarded the 1964 Nobel Peace Prize 43
Murders and Martyrs 44
   Deadly Church Bombing 45
   Three Civil Rights Workers Killed 46
   Civil Rights and Voting Rights Laws 46
   Big City Riots and Mayhem 47
   Black Power 47
   The Murder of Martin Luther King, Jr. 48
   The Murder of Robert Kennedy 49
Afterword: To Be Continued 50
Hate Crimes Today: An Age-old Foe in Modern Dress 51

About the Series

Researching American History is a series of books which introduces various topics and periods in our nation's history through the study of primary source documents.

Reading the Historical Documents

On the following pages you'll find words written by people during or soon after the time of the events. This is firsthand information about what life was like back then. Illustrations are also created to record history. These historical documents are called **primary source materials**.

At first, some things written in earlier times may seem difficult to understand. Language changes over the years, and the objects and activities described might be unfamiliar. Also, spellings were sometimes different. Below is a model which describes how we help with these challenges.

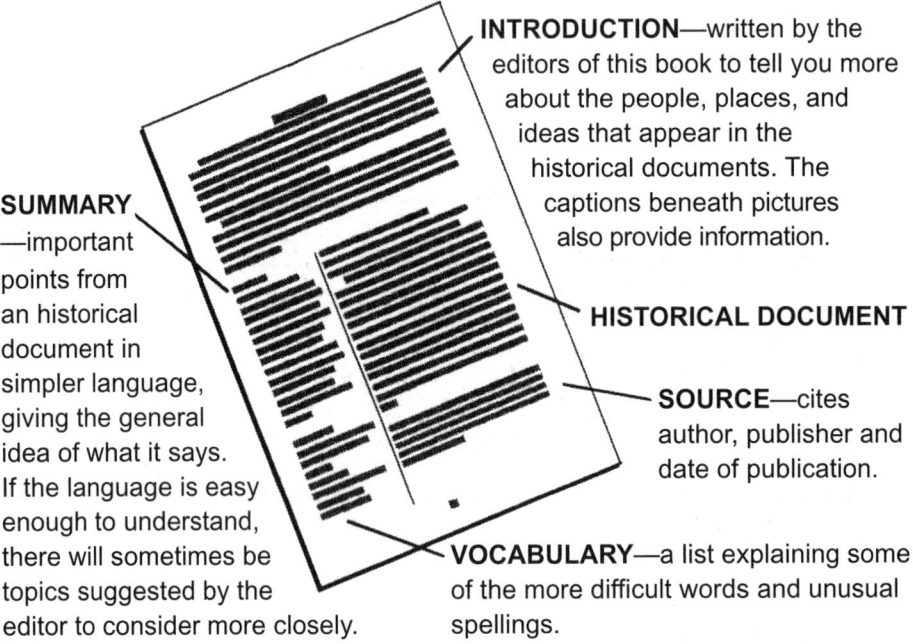

INTRODUCTION—written by the editors of this book to tell you more about the people, places, and ideas that appear in the historical documents. The captions beneath pictures also provide information.

SUMMARY—important points from an historical document in simpler language, giving the general idea of what it says. If the language is easy enough to understand, there will sometimes be topics suggested by the editor to consider more closely.

HISTORICAL DOCUMENT

SOURCE—cites author, publisher and date of publication.

VOCABULARY—a list explaining some of the more difficult words and unusual spellings.

In these historical documents, you may see three periods (…) called an ellipsis. It means that the editor has left out some words or sentences. You may see some words in brackets, such as [and]. These are words the editor has added to make the meaning clearer. When you use a document in a paper you're writing, you should include any ellipses and brackets it contains, just as you see them here. Be sure to give complete information about the author, title, and publisher of anything that was written by someone other than you.

Introduction: Civil Rights

The rights that a nation's people have by law are called civil rights. For example, civil rights include freedom of speech, press, assembly, the right to vote, freedom from involuntary servitude (slavery), and the right to equal treatment in public places. When anyone is denied such rights because of their particular class or group, that is called **discrimination**.

In 1864, the Thirteenth Amendment to the Constitution put an end to slavery, but some states passed "black codes" to limit the civil rights of freed slaves. In 1868, the Fourteenth Amendment declared that states could not limit the privileges of any general group of citizens. During the 20th century, many efforts were made to secure civil rights for African Americans. This period is generally called The Civil Rights Era, or the Civil Rights Movement.

Especially in the southern states, the races were usually kept separated. They used different public restrooms, restaurants, and drinking fountains. Signs were put up to say who could go where. African Americans and white people sat in different sections of buses (the blacks were in the back), movie theaters (blacks were often in the highest balcony), and in different bleachers at sporting events. In many cases, African Americans were simply not allowed in parks, swimming pools, and other recreational areas. This was considered normal. It was called **segregation**.

In 1896, Homer Adolph Plessy, who was an African American, challenged segregation in Louisiana. When Plessy was asked to leave a train coach reserved for white passengers, he refused. Under a Louisiana law requiring segregation on trains, Plessy was arrested and jailed. The case was argued in court, and eventually the U.S. Supreme Court upheld the Louisiana law. They said that "separate but equal" facilities were legal.

For many years, that Supreme Court decision allowed segregation to continue, even though facilities were almost never actually equal. Many opportunities were denied to African American citizens, and those who protested were treated brutally and sometimes murdered.

By the 1950s the Supreme Court and other federal courts began to declare segregation illegal. They required the equal availability—or **integration**—of facilities such as schools, buses, and restaurants.

In 1957, the Civil Rights Division of the Department of Justice was founded to enforce federal laws that forbid discrimination on the basis of race, sex, handicap, religion, and national origin.

Civil Rights Chronology

In this book, the events in the Civil Rights Movement are grouped according to the kind of effort involved (integrating education, obtaining voting rights, etc). This list places events in the order in which they happened, and shows you where to look for them.

1901 Mark Twain protests lynching, pp. 8-9
1904 Booker T. Washington protests lynching, p. 11
1910 NAACP founded, p. 16
1930s Black Muslims, Nation of Islam founded, p. 18
1939 Billie Holiday records "Strange Fruit," p. 12
1942 CORE founded (Chicago), p. 17
1947 Jackie Robinson breaks the color barrier in baseball, p. 13
1948 President Truman desegregates the military, p. 14

The Civil Rights Era

1954 May 17—Supreme Court rules on *Brown v. Board of Education* of Topeka, Kansas, declaring segregation in public schools unconstitutional, pp. 19–20

1955 December 1—Rosa Parks arrested for refusing to give up her seat to a white bus passenger (Montgomery, Alabama), p. 27

1956 Southern Congressmen sign a protest manifesto, p. 21
African Americans boycott buses (Montgomery, Alabama), pp. 28-29

1957 SCLC founded (Atlanta, Georgia), p. 16
September—White mobs prevent nine African American students from entering formerly all-white Central High School; President Eisenhower sends federal troops and the National Guard (Little Rock, Arkansas), pp. 22–25

1960 February 1—first sit-in when four African American college students are refused service at a Woolworth lunch counter (Greensboro, North Carolina), p. 32-37
April—SNCC founded (Shaw University, Raleigh, North Carolina), p. 17

1961   May 4—CORE , sends "freedom riders" to test laws against segregation in interstate travel, pp. 30-31

1962   James Meredith enrolls in the University of Mississippi, p. 26
COFO founded, p. 17

1963   June—Medgar Evers, Mississippi's NAACP field secretary murdered, p. 44
June—President Kennedy proposes Civil Rights Bill, p. 44
Freedom Marches, pp. 38-42
August 28—March on Washington; Martin Luther King, Jr. delivers "I Have a Dream" speech at the Lincoln Memorial, pp. 41-42
September 15—four young African American girls killed in a church bombing; in the hysteria that follows, two more young black people killed (Birmingham, Alabama), p. 45

1964   COFO sponsors drive to get African American voters registered, p. 46
July 2—President Johnson signs Civil Rights Act of 1964, making segregation in public facilities and discrimination in employment illegal, p. 46
August 5—Three civil-rights workers are declared missing, later discovered murdered, (Mississippi) p. 46
December 10—King awarded the Nobel Peace Prize, p. 43

1965   Race Riots break out in major northern and western cities, p. 47
August 21—Malcolm X murdered, (Harlem, New York), p. 47
March 7 "Bloody Sunday"— Police use tear gas, whips, and clubs on participants in voting-rights march (Selma, Alabama), p. 42
August 10—Voting Rights Act of 1965 passed by Congress, p. 46

1966   Black Panthers founded, p. 18

1968   April 4—Reverend Martin Luther King, Jr., assassinated (Memphis, Tennessee), pp. 48-49
April 11—Civil Rights Act of 1968 signed by President Johnson, prohibiting discrimination in housing, p. 46
June 5—Robert Kennedy assassinated (Los Angeles), p. 49

The Early 20th Century

Although the Civil War put an end to legal slavery, for many African Americans life didn't improve much. Living and working conditions in the late 1800s were sometimes nearly the same as they had been under slavery. In Southern states, organizations such as the Ku Klux Klan were determined to keep black people "in their place," by force. Organizations in northern states formed for similar purposes. Black homes were burned and black people were murdered.

Lynching

"Lynching" means putting someone to death by mob action, without legal process. The most popular means of lynching was hanging, and sometimes burning. Those thought to be outlaws were lynched on the western frontier, and immigrants were lynched in some cities. But most people lynched in America were African American men. Usually the lynch victim was accused of some crime, but he was killed by a mob, without any sort of legal procedure.

In the U.S., mobs lynched more than 4700 people between 1882 and 1968. More than 70 percent were African-Americans. By the early 20th century, 95 percent of lynchings were in the South. (Information from the Constitutional Rights Foundation, http://www.crf-usa.org/bria/bria10_3.html)

Mark Twain and Lyncherdom

The American author Samuel Clemens is better known by the name he used for his writing—Mark Twain. His famous stories and books such as *Life on the Mississippi, Tom Sawyer,* and *Huckleberry Finn* always included sharp observations on American life.

In 1900, lynching was on the increase in the Southern states. Twain hoped that this terrible crime would never happen in his home state of Missouri. But in 1901, it did. Deeply shocked, Twain wrote an essay called "The United States of Lyncherdom." The essay was never published during Twain's lifetime. When it was finally published in 1923, an editor changed some words to soften up Twain's bitterness. But it is still clear that Twain was trying to understand why human beings in a civilized country would do such a thing—and how those people could be changed.

On the following page is an excerpt from Mark Twain's essay.

Mark Twain Wonders Why

It has been supposed—and said—that the people at a lynching enjoy the spectacle and are glad of a chance to see it. It cannot be true; all experience is against it. The people in the South are made like the people in the North—the vast majority of whom are right-hearted and compassionate, and would be cruelly pained by such a spectacle—and would attend it, and let on to be pleased with it, if the public approval seemed to require it. …

It is thought, as I have said, that a lynching crowd enjoys a lynching. … If that were so, the crowds that saw the Windsor Hotel burn down would have enjoyed the horrors that fell under their eyes. Did they? … Many risked their lives to save the men and women who were in peril. Why did they do that? Because none would disapprove. There was no restraint; they could follow their natural impulse. Why does a crowd … pretend to enjoy a lynching? Why does it lift no hand or voice in protest? Only because it would be unpopular to do it, I think; each man is afraid of his neighbor's disapproval—a thing which, to the general run of the race, is more dreaded than wounds and death.

Source: Mark Twain, "The United States of Lyncherdom," 1901, published in Albert Bigelow Paine, *Europe and Elsewhere,* 1923. http://www.angelfire.com/mn3/mixed_lit/twain–lyncherdom.htm

Consider This:
What is the difference, according to Mark Twain, between people seeing others caught in a hotel fire and seeing a person lynched?

Why do you think that people behaved differently in those two cases?

Can you think of cases in your school or community when people simply did whatever would make them popular, even if they knew it was wrong?

Vocabulary:
compassionate = having feeling of sympathy for others

In "The United States of Lyncherdom," Mark Twain goes on to say that a "splendidly brave" person can stop the action of a mob. But, Twain warns, it takes more than physical bravery. And unfortunately, "There are not enough morally brave men in stock. We are out of moral-courage material; we are in a condition of profound poverty." In this book, you'll read about many cases of both physical and moral courage—where people did the unpopular thing.

Two Philosophies and Two Approaches

The struggle for Civil Rights in the early 20th century was led by two very different African Americans, each advocating his own approach to dealing with the issues and inequities faced by Blacks. Booker T. Washington favored practical education for Blacks and Native Americans, and believed they should focus their efforts on becoming self sufficient within their own communities.

Consider This:
Washington was not so concerned with social equality and its privileges. He was more interested in Blacks learning skills and trades by which they could earn a living. Many whites and blacks agreed. Why do you think they supported this philosophy?

From Booker T. Washington's "Atlanta Compromise" – 1895

The wisest among my race understand... social equality is the extremest folly, ... It is important and right that all privileges of the law be ours, but it is vastly more important that we be prepared for the exercises of these privileges. The opportunity to earn a dollar in a factory just now is worth infinitely more than the opportunity to spend a dollar in an opera-house.

Source: Booker T. Washington, *Up from Slavery,* (New York, 1901), pp. 224-25.

African American leader W.E.B. DuBois felt that Blacks could only gain equal rights and opportunities by fighting for integration and using all legal means available to do so, no matter how long it took.

Consider This:
In what ways do Washington's and DuBois' arguments differ?

Vocabulary:
bias = prejudice
barbarism = lacking refinement and education

Source: W.E. Burghardt DuBois, *The Souls of Black Folk,* (Chicago, 1903), pp. 54-7.

W.E.B. DuBois Responds

...[Negroes] do not expect that the free right to vote, to enjoy civic rights, and to be educated, will come in a moment; they do not expect to see the bias and prejudices of years disappear at the blast of a trumpet; but they are absolutely certain that the way for a people to gain their reasonable rights is not by voluntarily throwing them away and insisting that they do not want them; that the way for a people to gain respect is not by continually belittling and ridiculing themselves; that on the contrary, Negroes must insist continually, ...that voting is necessary to proper manhood, that color discrimination is barbarism, and that black boys need education as well as white boys....

Booker T. Washington was born into a slave family in 1856 but benefitted from emancipation. A leading advocate of vocational education, he established Tuskegee Institute and became a leading black conservative figure.

Booker T. Washington Protests

Booker T. Washington was born a slave, but after the Civil War he graduated from college, taught, and organized the Tuskegee Institute for African Americans. Washington became a well-known public speaker, and received honorary degrees from Dartmouth and Harvard. In February, 1904, he wrote the following letter, which was originally published in the *Birmingham Age-Herald*. The letter was also sent out by the Associated Press to other newspapers around the country.

A Protest

Within the last fortnight three members of my race have been burned at the stake; of these one was a woman.... All of these burnings took place in broad daylight and two of them occurred on Sunday afternoon in sight of a Christian church....

These burnings without a trial are in the deepest sense unjust to my race; but it is not this injustice alone which stirs my heart. These barbarous scenes ... are more disgraceful and degrading to the people who inflict the punishment than those who receive it....

Booker T. Washington.
Tuskegee, Ala., February 22, 1904.

Source: Booker T. Washington, "A Protest Against the Burning and Lynching of Negroes," *African American Perspectives: Pamphlets from the Daniel A.P. Murray Collection,* Library of Congress, http://memory.loc.gov

Consider This:
Why do you think Washington makes an issue of Christian churches?

Who is most disgraced by lynching, according to Washington? Why does he think so?

Vocabulary:
barbarous = uncivilized; very cruel
degrading = causing loss of status; humiliating
fortnight = 14 days
inflict = deal out; deliver by force

Billie Holiday

The Original Protest Song

In the mid-1930s, a New York schoolteacher named Abel Meeropol was upset at seeing a photo of a lynching. Using the pen name Lewis Allen, Meeropol wrote a song that he called "Bitter Fruit." In early 1939, he took his song to Billie Holiday, already a famous singer. When Holiday sang it in nightclubs, her audiences loved it. She also recorded the song as "Strange Fruit"—though her usual recording studio wouldn't touch it and she had to go with a smaller label. Even though the controversial piece was seldom played on the radio, it became a well-known and powerful protest song. (Information from www.wsws.org)

Consider This:
What do phrases like "Southern breeze," "poplar trees," and "pastoral scene" usually make you think of? What do they contrast with in this song?

Can you think of more recent protest songs? What kind of protest song could you write?

Vocabulary:
pastoral = relating to spiritual guidance; also relating to rural life

Strange Fruit

Southern trees bear a strange fruit,
Blood on the leaves and blood at the root,
Black body swinging in the Southern breeze,
Strange fruit hanging from the poplar trees.

Pastoral scene of the gallant South,
The bulging eyes and the twisted mouth,
Scent of magnolia sweet and fresh,
And the sudden smell of burning flesh.

Here is the fruit for the crows to pluck,
For the rain to gather, for the wind to suck,
For the sun to rot, for the tree to drop,
Here is a strange and bitter crop.

Robinson was the first black player in major league baseball in the modern era.

Breaking Baseball's Color Barrier

On April 10, 1947, an Associated Press newspaper story announced that "Jackie Robinson, brilliant Negro infielder, today became the first of his race to break into modern major league baseball when President Branch Rickey of the Brooklyn Dodgers announced the purchase of his contract from the Montreal Royals of the International League." National League president Ford Frick declared that Robinson "was the best player in our league last year." (Source: "Robinson Breaks Baseball's Color Barrier," Associated Press, April 10, 1947, http://wire.ap.org/APpackages/20thcentury/47robinson.html)

Death Threats

Never mind that Jackie Robinson was an exceptional athlete, some baseball fans and players were furious. Robinson was booed, cursed at, spat on, and intentionally "spiked" by other player's shoes. He received hate mail and death threats. In spite of that, he became an incredibly popular player, drawing crowds for his team. In 1962, Robinson was inducted into the Baseball Hall of Fame.

But Robinson wasn't the last African American baseball player to be threatened for being on a "white" team. Others, such as Willie Mays and Roy Campanella, also faced hostility. In 1974, Hank Aaron broke the home-run record set by white athlete Babe Ruth. Aaron received thousands of hate letters that threatened his life, and also threatened his family. Aaron went on to hit even more home runs and to break twelve other major league records. In 1969, Atlanta Braves fans voted Aaron the greatest player of all.

Announcement of Truman's desegregation order in a Chicago newspaper. (Chicago Defender, July 13, 1948)

Integrating the Military

In September, 1945, President Truman told Congress that "Every segment of our population, and every individual, has a right to expect from his government a fair deal." (Source: "Civil Rights Quotes," http://www.history-learningsite.co.uk/)

A few years later, Truman put an end to racial segregation in the military. His executive order set up a committee to carry out the desegregation of America's armed forces.

Vocabulary:
effectuate = cause
efficiency = ability to do something well
hereby = by this document
impairing = lessening the quality or efficiency
morale = level of confidence; optimism

Item #1 in Truman's Executive Order

…It is hereby declared to be the policy of the President that there shall be equality of treatment and opportunity for all persons in the armed services without regard to race, color, religion or national origin. This policy shall be put into effect as rapidly as possible, having due regard to the time required to effectuate any necessary changes without impairing efficiency or morale.…

Source: Harry S. Truman, Executive Order, July 26, 1948, "Establishing the President's Committee on Equality of Treatment and Opportunity in the Armed Services," http://lcweb.loc.gov/exhibits/odyssey

Ideas, Organizations, and People

In spite of breakthroughs in sports and in the military, progress toward racial equality was very slow. During the 1940s, 1950s, and 1960s, African Americans struggled constantly against the attitudes and laws that kept so many of them in poverty and in danger. They founded new organizations to coordinate their efforts. Brave new leaders—far too many to mention here—took up the struggle. This section covers a few of these ideas, groups, and leaders and tells where you can learn more about them.

James Lawson studied, practiced, and taught nonviolent protest—and he still does.

The Reverend Martin Luther King, Jr. (Seattle Times, November 1961)

Nonviolence

Mohandas Gandhi was a spiritual and political leader in India and South Africa in the late 19th and early 20th century. Gandhi gained civil rights for those who suffered discrimination by organizing nonviolent resistance to unjust laws. He became a model for many African Americans seeking change.

James M. Lawson, Jr., dedicated himself to nonviolence as a teenager. He served time in prison for refusing to cooperate with the draft during the Korean War. In 1953, Lawson went to India as a Methodist missionary. He was already an admirer of Gandhi, and his three years in India strengthened his belief in nonviolence. When Lawson returned to the U.S., he taught workshops in nonviolent techniques of resistance. Many who participated in the Civil Rights Movement were Lawson's students.

As a college and seminary student, Martin Luther King, Jr. was influenced by Thoreau's *Civil Disobedience* and by Gandhi's life, among other studies. In the early 1960s, King became pastor of a Baptist Church in Montgomery, Alabama. He was soon called upon to put his beliefs into action—and to teach an entire country what nonviolent resistance could accomplish.

In 1896, scholar and author W. E. B. Du Bois was the first African American to earn a Ph.D. from Harvard.

Julian Bond participated in sit-ins and protests. He served as a Georgia state representative and senator.

The NAACP

The National Association for the Advancement of Colored People was formed in 1910. After a 1908 lynching of two African Americans in Illinois, a white northerner called for a conference to discuss racial inequalities. The first African American member of the group was W. E. B. Du Bois. The NAACP grew out of those early meetings.

The NAACP Legal Defense and Education Fund is an independent branch that argues for civil rights in court. The NAACP and the Legal Defense and Education Fund helped bring about the 1954 Supreme Court ruling against segregation in public education.

Always in favor of nonviolent protests, the NAACP has been successful in many political efforts, including voter registration. Well known leaders in the organization have included Thurgood Marshall, Roy Wilkins, Benjamin Hooks, Merlie Evers-Williams (widow of slain civil-rights leader Medgar Evers), Julian Bond, and Representative Kweisi Mfume of Maryland. For more on the NAACP, see http://www.naacp.org

SCLC

During January, 1957, 60 people from 10 states attended a civil rights meeting in Atlanta, Georgia. In spite of a bombing—the home and church of African American Reverend Ralph David Abernathy—the organizers founded the Southern Leadership Conference. Officers included Martin Luther King, Jr. as president and Abernathy as financial secretary. In August 1957, the SLC changed its name to the Southern Christian Leadership Conference. The SCLC is dedicated to nonviolent mass action, and to keeping the movement open to all races and religions. For more, see http://sclcnational.org/

Andrew Young—a Congressman, U.S. Ambassador to the U.N., and Atlanta mayor—helped found the SCLC.

Jesse Jackson worked with the SCLC, then started additional food and voter registration programs.

SNCC

The Student Nonviolent Coordinating Committee was formed at Shaw University in Raleigh after the first North Carolina sit-ins. Members included the future Washington, D.C. mayor Marion Barry, Congressman John Lewis and NAACP chairman Julian Bond. SNCC (pronounced "snick") coordinated and publicized sit-ins, participated in freedom rides, and organized voter registration drives. At first, SNCC was dedicated to nonviolence. Later, under the leadership of Stokely Carmichael, SNCC became part of the Black Power movement. For more on SNCC, see http://www.ibiblio.org/sncc/index.html

CORE

The Congress of Racial Equality was founded in Chicago in 1942 by an interracial student group dedicated to nonviolent action for change. In the 1940s and again in the 1960s, CORE members organized lunch counter sit-ins and integrated bus rides. CORE has also focused attention to segregation in the North and West. For more about CORE, see http://www.core-online.org/

COFO

In 1962, with a $5,000 grant from the Voter Education Project, SNCC went into Mississippi to organize a voter registration drive. SNCC, SCLC, the Congress on Racial Equality (CORE), and the National Association for the Advancement of Colored People (NAACP) formed the Council of Federated Organizations (COFO), which launched the Freedom Vote campaign in 1963.

Muslim minister Malcolm X was a Black Power leader. He was assassinated in 1965, apparently by a rival.

Heavyweight boxing champion Muhammad Ali became a spokesman for black pride and accomplishment.

Black Nationalism and Black Power

In the mid-1960s, some civil rights movements emphasized African American self-reliance and pride. These groups supported social and economic separation from white society.

Black Muslims and the Nation of Islam

An African American religious movement based on Muslim principles was founded in the U.S. in the 1930s. In 1934, Elijah Muhammad became leader of the Nation of Islam, which emphasized African American separation from white society. Malcolm X., a Muslim minister, was suspended in 1963 because of differences with the leader. In 1964, world heavyweight boxing champion Cassius Clay joined the Nation of Islam and changed his name to Muhammad Ali. In 1977, a group of Black Muslims led by Louis Farrakhan split off from the original organization.

For more on the Nation of Islam, see http://www.noi.org/

Black Panthers

The largest organization for Black Power was the Black Panthers, a party founded in California in 1966 by Huey P. Newton and Bobby Seale. Eldridge Cleaver was a party official. The group originally supported violent revolution, and some members were involved in shoot-outs with police. Several were arrested on conspiracy charges, but were acquitted.

For more on the Black Panthers, see http://.blackpanther.org/

Desegregating Schools

In the early 1950s, racially segregated public schools were considered normal in most of America. All schools in a district—whether attended by African American children or by white children—were supposed to be equal. They almost never were. For example, in one South Carolina district all thirty of the school buses were used only by white students. Some black students walked nine miles to school. That county spent $179 per year on each white student, and $43 per year on each black student. And that kind of inequality wasn't limited to a single school district.

Brown v. Board of Education—1950–1954

Linda Brown was an African American third-grade student in Topeka, Kansas. She was not allowed to go to the elementary school that was seven blocks from her home, because that was for whites only. To get to her black school, she had to walk a mile through a dangerous railroad switchyard. The principal of a nearby white school refused to let Linda enroll there, so her father went to the local NAACP branch for help. The organization put Linda Brown's complaint together with several others, and took the case to court.

The Topeka Board of Education argued that segregated schools prepared black students for adulthood in the real world. The Board also claimed that segregation was not harmful. After all, they said, African Americans such as Frederick Douglass, Booker T. Washington, and George Washington Carver had achieved great things. The board didn't mention how difficult life had been for these exceptional men, or that Frederick Douglass had risked his life to escape from slavery.

But an 1896 Supreme Court decision called "Plessy v. Ferguson" had declared that separate but equal facilities were legal. Based on that, the Kansas court decided in favor of the Board of Education.

Brown and the NAACP appealed to the United States Supreme Court in October, 1951. Their case was combined with others from South Carolina, Virginia, and Delaware. The Supreme Court finally became convinced that segregation gave the black children a sense of inferiority that had a bad effect on their learning. The Court decided that separate schools could never be equal. In 1954, the Supreme Court ruled in favor of the plaintiffs, and declared that American schools must be desegregated.

 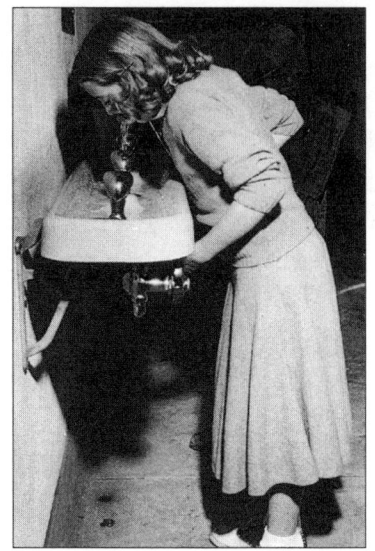

Obvious inequality of separate facilities made nonsense of the idea that segregation could be fair. (Photos by Ed Clark, *Life Magazine*, from *Constitution*, Spring 1989. Vol. 1/No. 3, p. 31)

Summary:
Does separating children in school only because of their race—even if the building and materials are equal—rob the minority of an equal chance for education? We believe so.

We have reached the decision that "separate but equal" has no place in public education. A separate education is always unequal.

Vocabulary:
conclude = judge
deprive = take away from
doctrine = rule; idea
facilities = things designed for a particular need
inherently = not possible to separate
tangible = physical

The Supreme Court Decision

Does segregation of children in public schools solely on the basis of race, even though the physical facilities and other "tangible" factors may be equal, deprive the children of the minority group of equal educational opportunities? We believe that it does...

We conclude that in the field of public education the doctrine of "separate but equal" has no place. Separate educational facilities are inherently unequal.

Source: Waldo Martin, *Brown v. Board of Education: A Brief History with Documents,* Boston: Bedford, 1998, pp. 173-74.

White Protest

The 1954 Supreme Court decision did not set a date for desegregating public schools, but it did put the process in motion. In 1956, more than ninety Southern Congressmen signed a protest manifesto.

Southern Manifesto

We regard the decision of the Supreme Court in the school cases as a clear abuse of judicial power.... This unwarranted exercise of power by the Court, contrary to the Constitution, is creating chaos and confusion in the States principally affected. It is destroying amicable relations between the white and Negro races that have been created through 90 years of patient effort by the good people of both races. It has planted hatred and suspicion where there has been heretofore friendship and understanding.

Without regard to the consent of the governed, outside agitators are threatening immediate and revolutionary changes in our public-school systems. If done, this is certain to destroy the system of public education in some of the States....

We commend the motives of those States which have declared the intention to resist forced integration by any lawful means....

We pledge ourselves to use all lawful means to bring about a reversal of this decision which is contrary to the Constitution and to prevent the use of force in its implementation.

In this trying period, as we all seek to right this wrong, we appeal to our people not to be provoked by the agitators and troublemakers invading our States and to scrupulously refrain from disorders and lawless acts.

Source: Waldo Martin, *Brown v. Board of Education: A Brief History with Documents,* Boston: Bedford, 1998, pp. 220-23.

Consider This:

What reasons does the manifesto give for not allowing integration?

One of the major reasons that some white people resisted integration—not given here—is that they were afraid of miscegenation (the mixing of the races). They thought that the white race should stay "pure."

Vocabulary:

agitators = those who try to arouse people's feelings for a cause
amicable = friendly
commend = praise
contrary = opposite to; in disagreement with
implementation = being put into effect
principally = first; most
revolutionary = new and different; causing great change
scrupulously = carefully; precisely
unwarranted = not justified

It was 1957 in Little Rock, Arkansas. Elizabeth Eckford was fifteen years old. On September 3, she wanted to enter Central High School, but National Guardsmen would not let her into the building. Hundreds of angry white people surrounded her. The mob screamed threats. Someone yelled, "Hang her!" An old woman spit on her. Finally a white woman got Elizabeth out of the mob and took her home on a city bus.

Integrating Central High

After the 1954 Supreme Court decision, the School Board of Little Rock, Arkansas outlined a gradual plan for integrating schools. The high school grades would be integrated first, beginning in September 1957. The school system was under court order to follow the schedule they had set for integration.

Finally the time came. Arkansas Governor Orval Faubus posted National Guard and State Police troops outside the formerly all white Central High School. The uniformed men had instructions to keep the peace. They closed nearby streets to traffic. When nine African American students came to register for classes, the National Guard turned them away.

Images of screaming white mobs surrounding black children appeared in newspapers and on television around the country.

A Central High Diary

Melba Patillo Beals was one of the African American students who helped to integrate Central High School. She kept a journal of her feelings and experiences. It was eventually published in her book, *Warriors Don't Cry*. On these pages are excerpts from Beals' book.

Warriors Don't Cry

I was disappointed not to see what is inside Central High School.

I don't understand why the governor sent grown-up soldiers to keep us out.

I don't know if I should go back.

But Grandma is right, if I don't go back, they will think they have won. They will think they can use soldiers to frighten us, and we'll always have to obey them. They'll always be in charge if I don't go back to Central and make the integration happen.

Source: Melba Patillo Beals, *Warriors Don't Cry*, New York: Washington Square Press, 1994, pp. 55-6.

Consider This:
Why did Melba think integration was important enough to put herself in danger?

The African American students sued Arkansas Governor Faubus to keep him from interfering with integration. The judge declared that integration of Central High School should proceed, and that the governor must not do anything to prevent it.

On September 23, the black students attended classes at Central High. National Guardsmen remained on the school grounds. Outside the school, a white mob still shouted angry words and slogans. Suddenly, the black students were called from their classes to the principal's office.

As I followed [my teacher] through an inner office past very official looking white men, I was alarmed by the anxious expressions on their faces .... I heard their frantic tone of voice, heard them say the mob was out of control, that they would have to call for help. "What are we gonna do about the nigger children?" asked one.

(Continued on next page)

Vocabulary:
frantic = feeling out of control with fear or worry
official = someone in a position of authority

Consider This:

Why do you think one voice that Melba heard suggested turning one child over to the mob?

What might have happened if that idea had been carried out?

Vocabulary:

barricades = something that blocks the way, set up for protection

raw-boned = rawboned; a lean person with prominent bones

"The crowd is moving fast. They've broken the barricades. These kids are trapped in here."

"Good Lord, you're right," another voice said. "We may have to let the mob have one of these kids, so's we can distract them long enough to get the others out."

"Let one of those kids hang? How's that gonna look? Niggers or not, they're children, and we got a job to do ......

"It may be the only way out. There must be a thousand people out there, armed and coming this way."

Then, I heard footsteps coming closer....

A tall, raw-boned, dark-haired man came toward us. "I'm Gene Smith, Assistant Chief of the Little Rock Police Department." He spoke in a calm tone. "It's time for you to leave for today. Come with me, now."

Source: Melba Patillo Beals, *Warriors Don't Cry,* New York: Washington Square Press, 1994, pp. 115-16.

Melba wrote that the Chief Smith inspired her confidence by the way he took charge. The black students got home safely that day.

By this time, President Eisenhower felt that he had to take action to prevent the Arkansas governor from ignoring court decisions. On September 24, Eisenhower called the Arkansas National Guard into active military duty, turning them into federal forces. He also authorized the use of the regular Army. Soon 1000 troops were stationed around Central High to protect the right of the black students to attend classes.

The African American students, now known as the Little Rock Nine, went back to school. Soldiers escorted them to classes and protected them at school. That didn't end all their problems. Some white students started being friendly, others continued to assault them. Three of the black students graduated from Central High and others graduated from other schools. The Little Rock Nine went on to universities and other advanced training, and succeeded in a variety of careers.

Central High School Newspaper

In 1957, *The Tiger* was Central High School's student newspaper. The paper calmly reported what was going on, explaining each step as it occurred. The following quotes are from an issue of *The Tiger*.

The Price We Pay
by Co-editors Georgia Dortch and Jane Emery

On the 25th of September, with few words and fixed bayonets, crack paratroopers of the U.S. Army quickly dispersed the crowds that had gathered around Central and carried out the court order for integration. No violent incidents, as had previously occurred, were reported.

No matter what our personal opinions may be, we cannot be proud of the violence that occurred around our school that made it necessary for the use of these Federal troops. Looking back on this year will probably be with regret that integration could not have been accomplished peacefully, without incident, without publicity.

But the future remains....

Let's Keep the Record Straight

Just for the sake of the record, let us remind our readers that less than 1% of the population of Little Rock was in the crowd of people gathered in front of CHS when school opened Monday morning, September 23. In addition to that, many of the people in the crowd were not citizens of Little Rock. There was at no time any significant disturbance in the classrooms of the high school....

Source: *The Tiger*, October 3, 1957, http://littlerock.about.com/gi/dynamic/offsite.htm?site=http://www.centralhigh57.org/the%5Ftiger.htm

Consider This:
According to these two stories, how were the Central High students different from the adults outside the school?

What do you think the student writers mean by their line, "But the future remains"?

What important comments do they make about the crowd?

Vocabulary:
accomplished = succeeded in doing something
dispersed = scattered and went away
fixed bayonets = blades that can be used for stabbing attached to the end of rifles
significant = large in amount; important

John Doar from the Justice Department and U.S. Marshall James McShane escort James Meredith to class. (Photo by Fred Ward, Black Star)

James Meredith in Mississippi

In 1962, Air Force Veteran James Meredith, who had already earned college credits, tried to enroll in the University of Mississippi. Meredith was turned away, but in September, 1962, a federal court ordered the university to accept him. The state's governor declared that he would never allow integration at the state-supported school. For days, white citizens rioted.

On October 1, Meredith was accompanied by federal officials as he enrolled for classes. He graduated the following August.

By 1966, Meredith thought that race relations in Mississippi were improving. He organized a "March Against Fear" from Memphis, Tennessee to Jackson, Mississippi.

A witness with the march reported hearing someone scream, "Look out!"

Commentary:
Although shot twice, Meredith recovered. Other civil rights leaders came and continued the march from the place that Meredith fell.

Meredith Struck Down

I turned and ... saw a man dressed in a white shirt and wearing sunglasses standing with a shotgun about 30 feet from a line of marchers ready to fire.

I saw James Meredith shove one of the marchers to the ground ... and I heard Meredith scream....

Source: "Look Out!" A Witness Account, Hernando, Miss., June 6 (AP), http://wire.ap.org/APpackages/20thcentury/66meredith.html

On December 1, 1955, seamstress Rosa Parks was riding the bus home from work in Montgomery, Alabama. According to city law, African Americans had to sit at the back of the bus. Parks sat toward the back, but when the bus filled up, the driver ordered her to give up her seat to a white man. Parks refused, and was arrested.(UPI)

Desegregating Transportation

After Rosa Parks was arrested, the African American community in Montgomery went into action. They distributed circulars and held meetings to discuss what actions they should take. The result was a boycott of the bus company. To many historians, this seems to be the moment that started the Civil Rights Movement.

Test of Segregated Transportation

MONTGOMERY, ALA.-The arrest of a Negro who refused to move to the colored section of a city bus may bring a court test of segregated transportation in the cradle of Confederacy....

Spokesmen ... said the boycott would continue until people who ride buses are no longer "intimidated, embarrassed and coerced."

Source: Rex Thomas, "Parks Arrested; Boycott Begins," Associated Press, December 5, 1955, http://wire.ap.org/APpackages/20thcentury/55busboycott.html

Vocabulary:
coerced = forced to do something against one's will

intimidated = made to be fearful

1956 Montgomery Bus Boycott

Originally supposed to be a one-day demonstration, the bus boycott continued for 381 days. Two-thirds of Montgomery bus riders were African Americans. Ninety percent of them refused to ride the buses. They got to work on foot, in private cars, in horse-drawn buggies, and even riding mules. The boycott ended on November 13, 1956, after a U.S. Supreme Court decision declared Montgomery's segregated bus seating unconstitutional.

Some white citizens of Montgomery also supported the bus boycott. White women drove their maids to and from work. The mayor of Montgomery published a list of white supporters, who also faced threats and sometimes the severe disapproval of their neighbors. In an interview for the PBS series *Eyes on the Prize,* Virginia Foster Durr and her husband, attorney Clifford Durr described those problems.

Consider This:

Can you think of other times or places when people did what they thought was right even when they knew they would suffer for it?

Have you or someone you know ever hesitated to do the right thing for fear of "being a social failure"?

Vocabulary:

boycott = the refusal to deal with a business or organization as a form of protest

White Supporters

The first thing that happened to whites like us who were sympathetic to the boycott was that we lost our businesses. People didn't come to us. We got a reputation. My husband got mighty little law business after he took a very decided stand. People like my husband and Aubrey Williams [publisher of the *Southern Farmer*] realized that they were cutting their own throats. Aubrey lost all of his advertising, every bit of it.

The fact that our family stood by us even though they did not agree with us was our salvation. If they had disowned us, had not stood by us, we could not have stayed....

There was another kind of terror. Some whites were scared that they wouldn't be invited to the ball, to the parties. It's a terror of being a social failure....

Source: Juan Williams, *Eyes on the Prize: America's Civil Rights Years, 1954-1965,* New York, Penguin, 1988, pp. 82-3.

Violence and Nonviolence in Montgomery

During the bus boycott, the African American community of Montgomery formed the Montgomery Improvement Association (MIA) to coordinate their efforts. A young pastor named Martin Luther King, Jr., was the first president of the MIA and Ralph David Abernathy was program director. At first, the group was supported by funds from church and meeting collections. But when the boycott appeared in the news, donations came in from all over the U.S. and even from other countries.

Many boycott leaders lost their jobs. Others faced violence and arrest. Black churches and homes were bombed and burned. One night while Martin Luther King, Jr. was speaking at a meeting, a bomb went off on the front porch. His home was partly destroyed, but King's family wasn't hurt.

Police, accompanied by Montgomery's mayor, rushed to the scene. But they quickly found themselves confronted by an angry African American crowd. King was already known for his support of nonviolence, and he stood by it that evening.

A Plea from King

"Please be peaceful," [King] said, standing on the shattered front porch. "We believe in law and order. We are not advocating violence. We want to love our enemies. If I am stopped, our work will not stop, for what we are doing is right. What we are doing is just—and God is with us."

Consider This:
Are these words typical for a man whose house has just been bombed?

Vocabulary:
advocating = supporting

To the relief of the white officials—who were greatly outnumbered—the crowd did as King asked. They broke up and went home.

A Policeman's Relief

"I'll be honest with you," said one policeman, "I was terrified. I owe my life to that nigger preacher, and so do all the other white people who were there."

Consider This:
Why does the policeman whose life was saved by King refer to him as a "nigger"?

Source: *I Have a Dream: the Story of Martin Luther King in Text and Pictures,* New York: Time-Life Books, 1968, p. 10.

Freedom Rides

A Supreme Court decision had outlawed segregated interstate buses in 1947. In 1960, the Court ruled that bus terminals on interstate routes could not be segregated. In 1961 CORE (see p. 18) organized a series of Freedom Rides to see if that decision was being carried out. A group of 14 people (seven black and seven white), including John Lewis, made the first of what would be many Freedom Rides.

Associated Press reporter Sid Moody reported that the riders "traveled a highway cobbled with blood and violence...." He mapped the rides, and noted where riders were arrested.

Sid Moody also noted where the riders faced violence: "On May 4 a freedom ride bus travelling from Washington, D.C., to New Orleans was burned near Anniston, Ala.... There were riots in Birmingham, Ala., which recurred on another ride two weeks later, spreading to Montgomery.... On June 13 four rabbis, seven white and seven Negro ministers staged a freedom ride from Washington to Tallahassee, Fla. They were jailed in Tallahassee after they were refused service at an airport restaurant...."

Source: Sid Moody, "Freedom Rides Brought More than Violence," report mailed to the Associated Press February 5, http://lcweb.loc.gov/exhibits/odyssey/archive/09/0904001r.jpg

Mob Violence Unchecked

Some of the worst violence against the Freedom Riders was in Alabama. The Justice Department later learned about a meeting of Ku Klux Klan officials in Birmingham. A paid FBI informer reported what a police official had told the Klan to do when the Freedom Riders got there.

Fifteen Minutes

"We're going to allow you fifteen minutes.... You can beat 'em, bomb 'em, maim 'em, kill 'em.... There will be absolutely no arrests. You can assure every Klansman in the country that no one will be arrested in Alabama for that fifteen minutes."

Source: David Halberstam, *The Children,* New York: Random House, 1998, p. 322.

Commentary:

This was not the only time that Southern police worked with the Klan to stop civil rights efforts.

Mobs in Montgomery

There was violence against the riders in Birmingham. The attack at the state capital, Montgomery, was even worse. When the Freedom Rider's bus reached Montgomery, everything was strangely quiet. Then the white mob struck. They beat up the journalists and destroyed their cameras. They beat the riders, especially going for the white supporters among them.

John Seigenthaler—the personal aide to Attorney General Robert Kennedy—was in Montgomery that day. He came to the bus terminal, not expecting any trouble. When he saw two young white women—Freedom Riders—being beaten, he helped them get into a taxi. But Seigenthaler was attacked and knocked unconscious. He had a fractured skull and broken ribs.

The mob was stopped by a white policeman named Floyd Mann, who fired his gun into the air, told the crowd there would be no killing that day, and held his gun on those who didn't want to quit.

Robert Kennedy sent 400 federal marshals to Montgomery to see that the violence was ended. After that, Attorney General Robert Kennedy and his brother, President John F. Kennedy, became more active in Civil Rights efforts. (Information from David Halberstam, *The Children,* New York: Random House, 1998, pp. 309–22).

After Birmingham and Montgomery, the country began to realize that the young African Americans of the South were putting their lives on the line every day for their beliefs, and for their rights.

Desegregating Public Dining

One of the many segregationist rules of southern society was that African Americans must stay out of restaurants that were owned by white people. In the case of nationwide chain stores, like F.W. Woolworth, African Americans could shop in all of the stores. In northern states, they were served at the Woolworth's lunch counter; in southern states they were not.

In Greensboro, North Carolina, for example, African Americans could buy food at a stand-up snack bar. But they were not allowed to eat at the long lunch counter, which featured stools with plastic cushions. Until 1958, the Greensboro store made everything clear with "colored only" and "whites only" signs. Even after those signs were protested and removed, black patrons kept to the areas traditionally open to them. This was also the practice in other southern stores with lunch counters.

On Feb. 1, 1960, four college freshmen bought toothpaste and school supplies in the Greensboro Woolworth's store. Then they went to the lunch counter, sat down, and ordered food. The clerk refused to serve them. They stayed until the store closed, and returned the next day. More black students joined them, sitting in and forming picket lines outside the store. The protest was quiet, and some students at the lunch counter spent their time at the counter studying.

Many newspapers and television stations covered the sit-ins. Finally, Woolworth and other chains agreed to integrate.

Activity:
Write in your own words a story about what these students were doing, and why.

North Carolina Sit-ins

A group of 20 Negro students from A&T College occupied luncheon counter seats, without being served, at the downtown F.W. Woolworth Co. Store late this morning....

Employes of Woolworth did not serve the group and they sat from 10:30 a.m. until after noon. White customers continued to sit and get service.

Source: Marvin Sykes, "Negro college students sit at Woolworth lunch counter," the *News & Record,* Tuesday, February 2, 1960, http://www.sitins.com/stories/main1960.htm News & Record

Looking Back Nearly Forty Years—
The story of the Greensboro Sit-ins

By Jim Schlosser

On Feb. 1, 1960, the Greensboro Four, as they would later be called, felt isolated and alone as they sat at that whites-only lunch counter at the Woolworth Store on South Elm Street.

They were seeking more than what they ordered—sodas, coffee, doughnuts. They were attacking the social order of the time. The unwritten rules of society required black people to stay out of white-owned restaurants, to use only designated drinking fountains and restrooms, to sit in the rear of Greensboro city buses, in a separate balcony at the Center Theatre and in segregated bleachers during sports events at War Memorial Stadium....

When the four men wouldn't budge from their seats, [the store manager] hurried to the police station two blocks away to see Chief Paul Calhoun. The unflappable chief said that as long as the students behaved, he could do nothing. He did dispatch a police officer to keep an eye on the store....

Then came a sign from heaven [according to one student]. An elderly white woman came up to them.

"She said, 'Boys, I am just so proud of you. My only regret is that you didn't do this 10 or 15 years ago,'" McCain recalls. "Well, 10 or 15 years ago, my goodness, I was only 8 or 10 years old, but I got the message and I can tell you that simple acknowledgment and pat on the shoulder meant more to me that day than anything else. ... I got so much pride and such a good positive feeling from that little old lady.

(Continued on next page)

Commentary:
This Woolworth store closed in 1995. Until then, a ceremony was held there every five years on February 1 to remember the sit-in. The Greensboro Four returned for the service. A vice president from Woolworth and Greensboro officials also always attended.

Vocabulary:
designated = chosen for a particular purpose
dispatch = send
isolated = alone; without support
unflappable = always able to stay calm

Franklin McCain, Joseph McNeil, Ezell Blair Jr., and David Richmond started the sit-in movement to integrate southern lunch counters and restaurants. They were all teenagers, college freshmen with academic scholarships at N.C. A&T State University. The sit-in lasted for five months, and led to end of segregated eating facilities at F.W. Woolworth and other chain stores.

Summary:
The counter from the Woolworth store where the sit-ins took place is now on display in the Smithsonian National Museum of American History.

Vocabulary:
deterred = discouraged from taking action

I mean, she'll never know it, but that really made the day for us."

Back from the police station, [the store manager] announced the store was closing early. The four students filed out, unserved but not deterred. They told Harris they would be back the next day....

Source: Jim Schlosser, "The story of the Greensboro Sit-ins," *The News & Record,* 1998. Posted by The Depot, http://www.sitins.com

Oliver W. Harrington. Dark Laughter. "My Daddy said they didn't seem to mind servin' him on the Anzio beach head. . ." Published in the Pittsburgh Courier, *April 2, 1960. Courtesy of Dr. Helma Harrington.*

When he was in grade school in the 1920s, Oliver W. Harrington (1912-1995) knew that he wanted to become a cartoonist. Even then, he drew caricatures (an image that exaggerates a person's features or personality). Harrington earned his Bachelor of Fine Arts degree from Yale. He moved away from the United States, but American newspapers continued publishing his cartoons about racism and injustice.

Diane Nash's Fear and Determination

Diane Nash grew up in Chicago, where she had simply ignored the hidden forms of discrimination she met. When she decided to go to college at Fisk University in Tennessee, she hadn't given much thought to the problem of segregation. The first time she ever saw "White Only" and "Colored" restroom signs was when a date took her to the Tennessee State Fair. When she began to notice things in downtown Nashville, she saw that black people sat on the sidewalk—rather than in a restaurant—to eat their lunches.

Nash became part of the Civil Rights movement in Tennessee. She took Jim Lawson's classes in nonviolent action, and was soon put in charge of organizing protests. Even though she seemed cool and calm to others, Diane Nash was always frightened. That didn't stop her.

In the 1960s, David Halberstam was a young reporter working in the South. He talked with Diane Nash and many other Civil Rights leaders. In his book *The Children* (New York: Random House, 1998) Halberstam tells the story of the sit-ins and freedom rides and marches that led to integration in the South. *The Children* opens with Diane Nash's description of being in class just before going to take her turn at a sit-in. She told Halberstam that she couldn't remember much of what the teacher said.

Consider This:
What does Diane Nash mean by "the clear handprint of her fear on the wooden desk"?

Vocabulary:
inability = lack of power to do something
colleagues = people one works with
steeled = braced; called up her determination

Remembering Fear

What she remembered ... was her fear. A large clock on the wall had clicked slowly and loudly; each minute which was subtracted put her nearer to harm's way. What she remembered about the class in the end was her inability to concentrate, and the fact that both her hands were soaked with sweat by the end of the class and left the clear handprint of her fear on the wooden desk. It was always the last class that she attended on the days that she and her colleagues assembled before they went downtown and challenged the age-old segregation laws at the lunch counters in Nashville's downtown shopping center. No matter how much she steeled herself, no matter how much she believed in what they were doing, the ... fear never left her....

Diane Nash Arrested

She was seated at a counter, and there was a cop, a rather pleasant one, actually, she decided, and he tried to be nice to her. He politely asked her and her friends to get up and they all refused. "Listen," he said, "if you don't get up you're going to be arrested," as if that were the most terrible warning imaginable, and upon hearing it, surely they would get up. The threat of arrest had probably always worked for him in the past. And these were, after all, well-dressed people, and the last thing well-dressed people would want was to go to jail. But no one moved. "All right, all right," he said, his patience quickly exhausted, "that's it! You've been warned! You're all under arrest!" They all got up, and as soon as they did, a dozen more of their colleagues came into the store and took their seats. The policeman seemed stunned: These young people wanted to be arrested. And when they got up, others took their places. After he helped arrest the second wave, a third wave took their seats. His face seemed to say it all–were they ever going to stop?

Source: David Halberstam, *The Children,* New York: Random House, 1998, p. 3 and pp. 133-34.

Commentary:

Whenever there was violence, the police arrested the African Americans for disturbing the peace. White attackers were not charged.

Many students who took part in the Nashville sit-ins would become well known in the Civil Rights Movement, including Diane Nash, John Lewis, James Bevel, and Marion Barry.

Vocabulary:

colleagues = people one works with

Birmingham cop sicks an attack dog on a demonstrator. (AP Wide World Photos)

Marching for Freedom

Sometimes people from African American communities organized marches to protest segregation in all its forms. In 1963, Martin Luther King, Jr. and the SCLC (p. 18) decided that it was time for a protest march in Birmingham, Alabama. They knew that the marchers would be met with violence and would be arrested. King enlisted 200 volunteers who were willing to go to jail. He held classes for them in nonviolent techniques, teaching them to accept blows without hitting back.

In April, a parade of well-dressed African American people marched through downtown Birmingham.

The Birmingham police chief, "Bull" Conner, had them arrested. More African Americans came to march. Conner had his men turn fire hoses and attack dogs on the marchers—while the whole world watched their televisions in horror.

More than 3,300 African Americans were arrested, including Martin Luther King. Black homes, businesses, and churches were bombed and burned.

African American children also joined the protest march, and about 2000 children were arrested.

A Third-Grader Goes to Jail

[We] marched about half a block. Then the police put us in paddy wagons, and we went to Juvenile Hall. There were lots of kids, but I think I may have been the youngest.... I was nine.... We slept in little rooms with bunk beds. There were about twelve of us in a room.... My parents could not get word to me for seven days.

Source: Audrey Faye Hendricks in *Freedom's Children: Young Civil Rights Activists Tell Their Own Stories*, The Children's Crusade, Turner Learning, Inc., 1999, http://www.turnerlearning.com/tntlearning/passing/historical.html

Consider This:
How would most third grader's react to being locked up away from their families for seven days?

Vocabulary:
paddy wagons = a police patrol wagon

Martin Luther King, Jr. on Why

While he was in jail in Birmingham, King wrote a letter to other clergymen who had criticized the protest march. They accused him of being an outsider coming to make trouble. King replied that the SCLC, of which he was president, had been invited to participate in a nonviolent program. But basically, King added, "I am in Birmingham because injustice is here...." Following are excerpts from his letter.

Letter from a Birmingham Jail
April 16, 1963
MY DEAR FELLOW CLERGYMEN:

... Perhaps it is easy for those who have never felt the stinging dark of segregation to say, "Wait." But when you have seen vicious mobs lynch your mothers and fathers at will and drown your sisters and brothers at whim; when you have seen hate-filled policemen curse, kick and even kill your black brothers and sisters; when you see the vast majority of your twenty

Summary:
Why do you think King describes segregation as the "stinging dark"?

Vocabulary:
vast = great number
whim = sudden idea; impulse

(Continued on next page)

Commentary:

In this same speech, King said, "We will have to repent in this generation not merely for the hateful words and actions of the bad people but for the appalling silence of the good people."

Activity:

Can you restate the above quote in your own words?

Vocabulary:

affluent = wealthy

distort = twist; tell in a misleading way

ominous = something that shows that something bad is going to happen

stance = attitude; view; position

---

million Negro brothers smothering in an airtight cage of poverty in the midst of an affluent society; when you suddenly find your tongue twisted and your speech stammering as you seek to explain to your six-year-old daughter why she can't go to the public amusement park that has just been advertised on television, and see tears welling up in her eyes when she is told that Funtown is closed to colored children, and see ominous clouds of inferiority beginning to form in her little mental sky, and see her beginning to distort her personality by developing an unconscious bitterness toward white people; … when you take a cross-county drive and find it necessary to sleep night after night in the uncomfortable corners of your automobile because no motel will accept you; when you are humiliated day in and day out by nagging signs reading "white" and "colored"; when your first name becomes "nigger," your middle name becomes "boy" (however old you are) … and your wife and mother are never given the respected title "Mrs."; when you are harried by day and haunted by night by the fact that you are a Negro, living constantly at tiptoe stance, never quite knowing what to expect next … then you will understand why we find it difficult to wait.....

Yours for the cause of Peace and Brotherhood,
MARTIN LUTHER KING, JR.

Source: The Martin Luther King, Jr. Papers Project at Stanford University, http://www.stanford.edu/group/King/liberation_curriculum/lesson_plans/lessonplans/king_crm_unit/handouts/letterfrombirmingham.html

Marchers filled the mall between the Lincoln Memorial and the Washington Monument on August 28, 1963. (Fred Ward Productions, Inc./ Black Star, 1963)

The March on Washington

Sit ins and demonstrations spread to the north. African Americans there wanted access to better jobs and better housing. Segregation wasn't the law in the north, but it was often the reality.

In August, 1963, about 250,000 marchers filled the area between the Lincoln Memorial and the Washington Monument. Martin Luther King, Jr. stood on the steps of the Lincoln Memorial and gave his most famous speech. He ended with his famous refrain "Free at last! Free at last! Thank God, almighty, we are free at last!"

"I have a dream…"

…that one day this nation will rise up and live out the true meaning of its creed: "We hold these truths to be self-evident; that all men are created equal."

Source: You can find the entire dream speech at The Martin Luther King, Jr. Papers Project at Stanford University, http://www.stanford.edu/group/King/publications/speeches/address_at_march_on_washington.pdf.

Consider This:
Do you know what else King said he dreamed of?
What are your own dreams for humanity?

Vocabulary:
creed = a set of beliefs

Martin Luther King, Jr. and Ralph Bunche were amongst the crowd of marchers in Selma, Alabama. (National Archives)

Marching for Voting Rights

In 1965, Martin Luther King, Andrew Young, and other civil rights leaders took part in a voting rights march in Selma, Alabama. King was put in jail, and another marcher was killed by police. On March 7, a march was planned from Selma to Montgomery. Leading the way were Hosea Williams of SCLC and John Lewis of SNCC. The day became known as "Bloody Sunday" when Alabama state troopers, many on horseback, attacked the 600 marchers with clubs and tear gas. On March 21, 25,000 activists—including many white northerners—successfully marched into Montgomery.

These young activists posed for the camera en route to Montgomery, Alabama. (Photo by Matt Heron/Black Star)

King Awarded the 1964 Nobel Peace Prize

In his Nobel acceptance speech, King said the award was a "recognition that nonviolence is the answer to the crucial political and moral question of our time—the need for man to overcome oppression and violence without resorting to violence and oppression…." (Source: http:/www.nobelprizes.com/nobel/peace/MLK-nobel.html) The next day, King gave his Nobel Lecture. Following are some excerpts.

The Quest for Peace and Justice

…Modern man has brought this whole world to an awe-inspiring threshold of the future. He has reached new and astonishing peaks of scientific success.…

Yet, in spite of these spectacular strides in science and technology, and still unlimited ones to come, something basic is missing. There is a sort of poverty of the spirit which stands in glaring contrast to our scientific and technological abundance. The richer we have become materially, the poorer we have become morally and spiritually. We have learned to fly the air like birds and swim the sea like fish, but we have not learned the simple art of living together as brothers.…

Source: Martin Luther King, Nobel Lecture, December 11, 1964, http://www.nobel.se/peace/laureates/1964/king-lecture.html

Consider This:
In his Nobel lecture, King discussed "three larger problems which grow out of man's ethical infantilism." The problems he listed are "racial injustice, poverty, and war."

What do you think are humanity's major problems today?

Vocabulary:
abundance = plenty of
technological = using machines and tools
threshold = entrance; point where something new begins

Murders and Martyrs

Many participants in the Civil Rights Movement were killed—at least 40 between 1954 and 1958. Some were deliberately targeted for their activities. Others were killed simply because they were black, or were white and working with black people. No one was ever charged for most of the murders, even though there were many witnesses in some cases.

The victims include: Lamarr Smith, 1955, shot because he registered to vote and urged others to register; Emmett Till, 1955, hanged because he supposedly flirted with a white woman; Corporal Roman Ducksworth, Jr, 1962, on his way south from Maryland to visit his sick wife, was ordered off a bus and shot by the driver. (Information from "The Civil Rights Martyrs," http://www.preservice.org/T0300238/crMartyrs.htmtyrs)

In June 1963, the Mississippi field secretary for the NAACP was murdered outside of his home by a sniper. In 1994, Byron de la Beckwith was convicted of the murder and given a life sentence.

On June 11, 1963, President John F. Kennedy proposed a Civil Rights Bill. He made a televised speech asking the nation to live up to its ideals.

Consider This:

Hypocrisy means pretending to have admirable aims when you really don't. In this speech, President Kennedy pointed out the hypocrisy of a government saying good things but not applying them to all citizens.

Can you think of examples of hypocrisy from your own experience.

President Kennedy on Civil Rights

We preach freedom around the world, and we mean it, and we cherish our freedom here at home, but are we to say to the world, and much more importantly, to each other that this is the land of the free except for the Negroes; that we have no second class citizens except Negroes; that we have no class or caste system, no ghettoes, no master race except with respect to Negroes?

Now the time has come for this Nation to fulfill its promise....

Source: Thomas West and James Monney, eds., *To Redeem a Nation: A History and Anthology of the Civil Rights Movement,* St. James: Brandywine Press, 1993, pp. 164-65.

Deadly Church Bombing

In September, 1963, a bomb exploded in an African American Baptist church in Birmingham, Alabama. Inside were 400 people, including 80 children. The blast killed four young girls—ages 10 to 14—and injured many others. Attorney General Robert F. Kennedy rushed in 25 FBI agents, including bomb experts. The bombing was the 21st in Birmingham in eight years, and the fourth in the last four weeks. None of the bombers had been caught.

In 1977, Robert Edward Chambliss was convicted of murder in the church bombing. In 1997, the FBI reopened its investigation. Several years later, former Ku Klux Klan members Thomas Blanton Jr. and Bobby Frank Cherry were convicted of first-degree murder and jailed.

Six Dead After Church Bombing

Birmingham, Sept. 15 — A bomb hurled from a passing car blasted a crowded Negro church today, killing four girls in their Sunday school classes and triggering outbreaks of violence....

Dozens of survivors, their faces dripping blood from the glass that flew out of the church's stained glass windows, staggered around the building in a cloud of white dust raised by the explosion. The blast crushed two nearby cars like toys and blew out windows blocks away....

Commentary:
The death of these children shocked many people around the country and around the world. Still, it was many years before those who did it were brought to justice.

Hysteria followed: shots were fired, five black businesses were burned, and about 2000 African Americans rioted. City police, State Troopers, and National Guardsmen tried to keep order. But some law officers panicked.

City police shot a 16-year-old Negro to death when he refused to heed their commands to halt after they caught him stoning cars. A 13-year-old Negro boy was shot and killed as he rode his bicycle in a suburban area north of the city....

Source: The Washington Post/United Press International September 16, 1963, TNT— Segregation In America
http://www.washingtonpost.com/wp-srv/national/longterm/churches/photo3.htm

Consider This:
Why do you think that this additional violence followed the bombing?

Three Civil Rights Workers Killed

In 1964, COFO used northern volunteers in a major drive to register African American voters in the South. In June, three workers in Mississippi—Michael Schwerner, Andrew Goodman and James Earl Chaney—were arrested, then released, and then reported missing. Their buried bodies were found five weeks later. An investigation discovered that deputies had notified the Ku Klux Klan when the workers were about to be released. The sheriff, a deputy, and 17 other men were convicted of federal conspiracy charges in connection with the murders. A 1988 movie, "Mississippi Burning," is based on these events.

Lyndon Johnson signs the Voting Rights Act of 1964, while Martin Luther King, Jr. looks on. (National Archives)

Civil Rights and Voting Rights Laws

On November 22, 1963, President John F. Kennedy was assassinated in Dallas, Texas. As the nation mourned Kennedy's death, Vice President Lyndon B. Johnson became president. Johnson had known poverty and had seen racism up close. He wanted to do away with both.

President Johnson pushed the Civil Rights Act of 1964 through Congress. The new law made it illegal for any business open to the public—even if it was privately owned—to turn away customers because of their race. It banned the hiring or firing of employees because of race.

Johnson promoted and signed other civil rights measures: the Voting Rights Act of 1965, making it easier for African Americans to register to vote; and the Civil Rights Act of 1968, outlawing discrimination in housing rentals, sales, and financing.

Big City Riots and Mayhem

Although segregation wasn't the law outside of the South, racism could be just as strong in the North and West. The unemployment rate for African Americans was double that for white workers. Many black families lived in ghettoes where crime and violence were high. In the 1960s, their frustration exploded into violence—rioting, burning, and looting—in several major cities.

In 1965, the Los Angeles Watts neighborhood exploded, and rioting went on for six days. Rudy Washington lived in Watts and saw it all happen.

A 14-year-old in Watts

"I could sit on my porch and listen to the windows breaking. At the time, there was a place around the corner from me on 120th called Shop-Rite. The drug store was there and I ... could sit on my front porch and [watch] people running up and down my street with couches and televisions.... As a child I saw the whole thing transpire. I watched the police come, the National Guard. I watched the looting. I watched the killings. That was at 14...."

Source: Found at http://www.irn.pdx.edu/~strukn/Watts/riot.htm

Activity:
Write a speech or story from the point of view of the young teenager watching the riots.

Vocabulary:
transpire = take place

Black Power

Nonviolent protests gave way to other points of view. Many African Americans struggled to gain control over their own black communities. Some were in favor of complete separation from white communities.

The Black Panthers and other groups began arming themselves and patrolling African American neighborhoods.

The SNCC organization expelled its white members and turned away from the group's nonviolent origins.

On August 21st, 1965, Malcolm X was murdered, apparently by rivals within the Black Power movement.

The Murder of Martin Luther King, Jr.

On April 4, 1968, a sniper shot Martin Luther King, Jr. as he stood on his hotel balcony. King, who was just 39, died almost immediately. The nation reacted with shock, anger, and with pleas that King's belief in nonviolence would be honored. Riots again broke out in some cities.

James Earl Ray was arrested for the crime. He confessed, was convicted, and was sentenced to life in jail. Ray later denied his confession, spinning a number of conspiracy stories about what happened. In 1998, Ray died in jail, leaving many questions unanswered.

Commentary:
In a terrible irony, the American who most promoted change by nonviolent means was violently murdered. Irony is a contrast or mismatch between appearance and reality. This type of irony is called situational irony—in which something happens that is the opposite of what should be expected.

Commentary:
The Associated Press website includes quotes from many other people who knew or admired King: http://wire.ap.org/APpackages/20thcentury/68kingassassinated.html

Dr. Martin Luther King Jr. Assassinated

MEMPHIS, TENN. (AP) - Nobel Laureate Martin Luther King Jr., father of nonviolence in the American civil rights movement, was killed by an assassin's bullet....

The 1964 Nobel Peace Prize winner was standing on the balcony of his motel here, where he had come to lead protests in behalf of the city's 1,300 striking garbage workers, most of them Negroes, when he was shot....

Source: Associated Press, http://wire.ap.org/APpackages/20thcentury/68kingassassinated.html

A Stunned Nation
By Brian Sullivan

NEW YORK ..."We have been saddened," President Johnson told the nation on radio and television....

Mrs. Rosa Parks ... wept at her Detroit home: "I can't talk now, I just can't talk."...

Jackie Robinson...: "I'm shocked. Oh, my God, I'm frightened. I'm very concerned, disturbed and very worried. I pray God this doesn't end up in the streets."

Source: Associated Press, http://wire.ap.org/APpackages/20thcentury/68kingassassinated.html

Robert Kennedy about King

...Martin Luther King dedicated his life to love and to justice for his fellow human beings, and he died because of that effort.

In this difficult day, in this difficult time for the United States, it is perhaps well to ask what kind of a nation we are and what direction we want to move in....

What we need in the United States is not division; what we need in the United States is not hatred; what we need in the United States is not violence or lawlessness; but love and wisdom, and compassion toward one another, and a feeling of justice toward those who still suffer within our country, whether they be white or they be black....

We can do well in this country. We will have difficult times; we've had difficult times in the past; we will have difficult times in the future. It is not the end of violence; it is not the end of lawlessness; it is not the end of disorder.

But the vast majority of white people and the vast majority of black people in this country want to live together, want to improve the quality of our life, and want justice for all human beings who abide in our land....

Source: Kennedy Speech on Martin Luther King, Jr.'s Death, April 4, 1968, Indianapolis, Indiana, http://members.iquest.net/~reboomer/kensp.htm

Commentary:

Martin Luther King's death was especially horrifying for the civil rights leaders who had worked with him and admired him. One of those leaders was John Lewis.

In 1968, Lewis was working for Robert Kennedy's presidential campaign. When King was assassinated, Lewis was nearly overwhelmed with shock. But Lewis felt that some hope for the movement still remained if Kennedy gained power. But Kennedy was the next one to fall.

Vocabulary:
abide = live
compassion = sympathy for the suffering of others

The Murder of Robert Kennedy

On June 5, 1968, Robert Kennedy won the California primary for the Democratic candidate for President of the United States. When he went downstairs in his Los Angeles hotel to make his acceptance speech, Kennedy was shot and killed.

The shooter, Sirhan Sirhan, is serving a life sentence for the murder.

Afterword: To Be Continued

In a 2001 broadcast on National Public Radio, *Newsweek Magazine* editor Jon Meacham commented on the courage shown by civil rights leaders.

> ...Unless we understand that the movement was not a sure thing, we can't really appreciate the courage it took for people like John Lewis and countless others to march in the streets and change a nation's habit of hearts and minds. It's remarkable to think that this was all just the day before yesterday....

During the 20th century, U.S. citizens began to realize that civil rights must be extended to others who had also experienced discrimination: people of other nationalities, such as the Japanese during World War II, Mexicans and other immigrants, and American Arabs and other Muslims; women, who finally got the right to vote in 1920, and who still struggle for equal job opportunities; and people with handicaps or with non-traditional lifestyles and sexual preferences. Meacham was talking about the African American Civil Rights Movement, but his words apply to all our civil rights, and to all our responsibilities:

> We have quite a ways to go, but, you know, America is a work in progress. We have made tremendous progress. We have to become more comfortable with our diversity and accept the fact that we're en route to becoming the most diverse nation in the history of humankind. And we have to come terms with that....
>
> I think Dr. King merely charted a course. He didn't lead us all the way there. And it's actually incumbent on all of us and not just a select few to make sure that happens.
>
> Source: Frank Stasio, "Analysis: Civil rights struggles in America, past, present and future," *Talk of the Nation (NPR),* January 15, 2001.

"Hate Crimes Today: An Age-old Foe in Modern Dress"

The Special Nature of an Extreme Expression of Prejudice

Hate crimes—violent acts against people, property, or organizations because of the group to which they belong or identify with—are a tragic part of American history. However, it wasn't until early in this decade that the federal government began to collect data on how many and what kind of hate crimes are being committed, and by whom. Thus, the statistical history on hate crimes is meager. Psychological studies are also fairly new. Nevertheless, scientific research is beginning to yield some good perspectives on the general nature of crimes committed because of real or perceived differences in race, religion, ethnicity or national origin, sexual orientation, disability, or gender.

According to the FBI, about 30% of hate crimes in 1996, the most recent year for which figures are available, were crimes against property. They involved robbing, vandalizing, destroying, stealing, or setting fire to vehicles, homes, stores, or places of worship.

About 70% involve an attack against a person. The offense can range from simple assault (i.e., no weapon is involved) to aggravated assault, rape, and murder. This kind of attack takes place on two levels; not only is it an attack on one's physical self, but it is also an attack on one's very identity.

Who commits hate crimes?

Many people perceive hate crime perpetrators as crazed, hate-filled neo-Nazis or "skinheads". But research by Dr. Edward Dunbar, a clinical psychologist at the University of California, Los Angeles, reveals that of 1,459 hate crimes committed in the Los Angeles area in the period 1994 to 1995, fewer than 5% of the offenders were members of organized hate groups.

Most hate crimes are carried out by otherwise law-abiding young people who see little wrong with their actions. Alcohol and drugs sometimes help fuel these crimes, but the main determinant appears to be personal prejudice, a situation that colors people's judgment, blinding the aggressors to the immorality of what they are doing. Such prejudice is most likely rooted in an environment that disdains someone who is "different" or sees that difference as threatening....

. . . .

Researchers have concluded that hate crimes are not necessarily random, uncontrollable, or inevitable occurrences. There is overwhelming evidence that society can intervene to reduce or prevent many forms of violence, especially among young people, including the hate-induced violence that threatens and intimidates entire categories of people.

How much hate crime is out there?

Educated "guesstimates" of the prevalence of hate crimes are difficult because of state-by-state differences in the way such crimes are defined and reported. Federal law enforcement officials have only been compiling nationwide hate crime statistics since 1991, the year after the Hate Crimes Statistics Act was enacted. Before passage of the act, hate crimes were lumped together with such offenses as homicide, assault, rape, robbery, and arson.

In 1996, law enforcement agencies in 49 states and the District of Columbia reported 8,759 bias-motivated criminal offenses to the Federal Bureau of Investigation, the federal government agency mandated by Congress to gather the statistics. However, points out the FBI, these data must be approached with caution. Typically, data on hate crimes collected by social scientists and such groups as the Anti-Defamation League, the National Asian Pacific American Legal Consortium, and the National Gay and Lesbian Task Force show a higher prevalence of hate crime than do federal statistics.

The Hate Crimes Prevention Act of 1998, introduced in both the House (H.R. 3081) and Senate (S. 1529), seeks to expand federal jurisdiction over hate crimes by (1) allowing federal authorities to investigate all possible hate crimes, not only those where the victim was engaged in a federally protected activity such as voting, going to school, or crossing state lines; and (2) expanding the categories that are currently covered by hate crimes legislation to include gender, sexual orientation, and disability.

....

...[An]obstacle to gaining an accurate count of hate crimes is the reluctance of many victims to report such attacks. In fact, they are much less likely than other victims to report crimes to the police, despite-or perhaps because of-the fact that they can frequently identify the perpetrators. This reluctance often derives from the trauma the victim experiences, as well as a fear of retaliation.

....

What is the emotional damage?

Intense feelings of vulnerability, anger, and depression, physical ailments and learning problems, and difficult interpersonal relations—all symptoms of posttraumatic stress disorder—can be brought on by a hate crime.

Dr. Herek and his colleagues found that some hate crime victims have needed as much as 5 years to overcome their ordeal. By contrast, victims of nonbias crimes experienced a decrease in crime-related psychological problems within 2 years of the crime. Like other victims of posttraumatic stress, hate crime victims may heal more quickly when appropriate support and resources are made available soon after the incident occurs.

Why do people commit hate crimes?

Hate crimes are message crimes, according to Dr. Jack McDevitt, a criminologist at Northeastern University in Boston. They are different from other crimes in that the offender is sending a message to members of a certain group that they are unwelcome in a particular neighborhood, community, school, or workplace.

Racial hatred

By far the largest determinant of hate crimes is racial bias, with African Americans the group at greatest risk. In 1996, 4,831 out of the 7,947 such crimes reported to the FBI, or 60%, were promulgated because of race, with close to two-thirds (62%) targeting African Americans. Furthermore, the type of crime committed against this group has not changed much since the 19th century; it still includes bombing and vandalizing churches, burning crosses on home lawns, and murder.

Among the other racially motivated crimes, about 25% were committed against white people, 7% against Asian Pacific Americans, slightly less than 5% against multiracial groups, and 1% against Native Americans and Alaskan Natives.

Resentment of ethnic minorities

Ethnic minorities in the United States often become targets of hate crimes because they are perceived to be new to the country even if their families have been here for generations, or simply because they are seen as different from the mainstream population. In the first case, ethnic minorities can fall victim to anti-immigrant bias that includes a recurrent preoccupation with "nativism" (i.e., policies favoring people born in the United States), resentment when so-called "immigrants" succeed (often related to a fear of losing jobs to newcomers), and disdain or anger when they act against the established norm. In the second case, negative stereotypes of certain ethnic groups or people of a certain nationality can fuel antagonism.

Hispanics.

People from Latin America are increasingly targets of bias-motivated crimes....

Attacks on Hispanics have a particularly long history in California and throughout the Southwest where, during recurring periods of strong anti-immigrant sentiment, both new immigrants and long-time U.S. citizens of Mexican descent were blamed for social and economic problems and harassed or deported en masse.

Asian Pacific Americans.

Bias against Asian Pacific Americans, which is increasing today, is long-standing. The Chinese Exclusion Act passed in 1882 barred Chinese laborers from entering this country.... The act was not repealed until 1943. Moreover, although the act specifically referred to the Chinese, Japanese people were also affected because most people could not tell the two groups apart. To this day, according to the Leadership Conference on Civil Rights, hostility against one Asian Pacific American group can spill over onto another.

....

...The Leadership Conference on Civil Rights and other experts in the field find that present-day resentment is frequently fueled by the stereotype that Asian Pacific Americans are harder-working, more successful academically, and more affluent than most other Americans.

Arab Americans.

Another growing immigrant group experiencing an upsurge in hate crime, largely as a result of Middle East crises and the September 11, 2001 terrorist attacks, are people of Arab descent. Often they are blamed for incidents to which they have no connection. The hate crimes following the 9/11 terrorist attacks, which included murder and beatings, were directed at Arabs solely because they shared or were perceived as sharing the national background of the hijackers responsible for attacking the World Trade Center and the Pentagon.

Religious discrimination

Most religiously motivated hate crimes are acts of vandalism, although personal attacks are not uncommon. The overwhelming majority (82% in 1996) are directed against Jews, states the FBI. The 781 acts of vandalism that year represent a 7% increase from 1995. However, acts of harassment, threat, or assault went down by 15%, to 941, from a total of 1,116, a decline that the Anti-Defamation League attributes to stronger enforcement of the law and heightened educational outreach.

....

People of other religions in the United States also experience hate crimes. The FBI reported a seventeen-fold increase in anti-Muslim crimes nationwide during 2001, largely due to the 9/11 terrorist attacks. Muslims were also victims of harassment in the period immediately following the bombing of the Murrah federal building in Oklahoma City;....

Gender-based bias

Gender-based violence is a significant social and historical problem, with women the predominant victims. Only recently, however, have these acts of violence been characterized as hate crimes. The Hate Crimes Prevention Act of 1998 would make gender a category of bias-motivated crime....

....

The more violence a woman experiences, the more she suffers from psychological distress that spills over into many areas of life. Most violence against women is not committed during random encounters but by a current or former male partner. Exposed to attacks and threats over and over again, victims often live with increasing levels of isolation and terror. Typical long-term effects of male violence in an intimate adult relationship are low self-esteem, depression, and posttraumatic stress disorder....

Disdain of gay men and lesbians

The most socially acceptable, and probably the most widespread, form of hate crime among teenagers and young adults are those targeting sexual minorities, says Dr. Franklin. She has identified four categories of assaulters involved in such crimes, as follows:

* Ideology assailants report that their crimes stem from their negative beliefs and attitudes about homosexuality that they perceive other people in the community share. They see themselves as enforcing social morals.
* Thrill seekers are typically adolescents who commit assaults to alleviate boredom, to have fun and excitement, and to feel strong.
* Peer-dynamics assailants also tend to be adolescents; they commit assaults in an effort to prove their toughness and heterosexuality to friends.
* Self-defense assailants typically believe that homosexuals are sexual predators and say they were responding to aggressive sexual propositions.

Lesbian and gay victims suffer more serious psychological effects from hate crimes than from other kinds of criminal injury. In their case, the association between vulnerability and sexual orientation is particularly harmful. This is because sexual identity is such an important part of one's self-concept...

Scorn of people with disabilities

Congress amended the Hate Crimes Statistics Act in 1994 to add disabilities as a category for which hate crimes data are to be collected. Because the FBI only began collecting statistics on disability bias in 1997, results are not yet available. However, we know from social science research that the perva-

(Continued on next page)

sive stigma that people apply to both mental and physical disability is expressed in many forms of discriminatory behaviors and practices, including increased risk for sexual and physical abuse.

The Judge David L. Bazelon Center for Mental Health Law, a national organization representing low-income adults and children with mental disabilities, holds that such hate crimes are motivated by the perception that people with disabilities are not equal, deserving, contributing members of society, and, therefore, it is okay to attack them.

Does the economy play a part?

...one form of economic change that may set the stage for racist hate crimes occurs when minorities first move into an ethnically homogeneous area. According to Dr. Green, the resulting violent reaction seems to be based on a visceral aversion to social change. The offenders frequently justify the use of force to preserve what they see as their disappearing, traditional way of life. The more rapid the change, holds Dr. Green, the more likely violence will occur...

Is there something we can do?

....

* Support programs that offer training for police and victim-assistance professionals on early intervention techniques that help hate crime victims better cope with trauma. The curriculum could be similar to one developed by the CRS.
* Encourage communities to launch educational efforts aimed at dispelling minority stereotypes, reducing hostility between groups, and encouraging broader intercultural understanding and appreciation. Specifically, according to Dr. Franklin, it is important that school administrators, school boards, and classroom teachers constantly confront harassment and denigration of those who are different. Antibias teaching should start in early childhood and continue through high school. Teachers must also know that they have the backing of administrators and school board members to intervene against incidents of bias whether inside the school or on the playground.

For more information, contact the following organizations.

The Community Relations Service, Department of Justice, is the only federal agency whose primary task is to help communities respond appropriately to organized hate groups. It was created by the Civil Rights Act of 1964. CRS helps prevent and resolve communitywide conflict stemming from race, color, and national origin. Community Relations Service (CRS), U.S. Department of Justice, Second and Chestnut Street, #208, Philadelphia, PA 19106

Source: PsychNET®; ©1998. American Psychological Association, Washington, DC